ORGASM: OVER 100 TRULY EXPLOSIVE TIPS

THIS IS A CARLTON BOOK

Text and design copyright © 2001 Carlton Books Limited
This edition published by Carlton Books Limited 2001
20 Mortimer Street, London W1T 3JW

A CIP catalogue record for this book is available from the
British Library.
ISBN 1 84222 153 1

Printed in Singapore

Editorial Manager: Venetia Penfold
Art Director: Penny Stock
Editor: Jane Donovan
Design: DW Design
Production Manager: Garry Lewis

ORGASM: OVER 100 TRULY EXPLOSIVE TIPS

LISA SUSSMAN

CARLTON
BOOKS

OOOOHH!

SECTION ONE

ORGASM TRAINING TIPS

According to sex pros Masters and Johnson, 10 per cent of women have never experienced the melting sensation of the Big O. But that doesn't mean they're ice queens. After all, orgasms aren't a basic instinct; they're a learned technique. Here are some sexercises that'll make you moan with delight:

1 **Masturbation** is the surest path to orgasm for both sexes — most people can bring themselves to ecstasy in four minutes flat. And research shows that the more orgasms you have by any means, the more orgasms you will have overall. Women who regularly let their fingers do the walking require less time to become aroused, have significantly more orgasms, greater sexual desire, higher self-esteem and greater marital and sexual satisfaction.

PRACTISE, PRACTISE, **PRACTISE**

2

Sex is like any other exercise. The more you do it, the better you become at it and the more you will enjoy it – the chemicals in your brain guarantee this. If you start making love more often, the chemical communication between brain cells quickens and intensifies because the impulses are travelling on a well-beaten path. The pay-off is more orgasms with less effort.

3

One fact that was probably left out of your biology class was the 'Use It' or 'Lose It' theory of sex.

Sexual abstinence in women causes what's known as **'vaginal atrophy'** – a general drying and closing-up of the vagina to the point where intercourse becomes virtually impossible. But studies have shown that women who stay sexually active, either with a partner or through self-stimulation, clock in more orgasms.

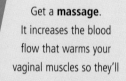

Get a **massage**.
It increases the blood
flow that warms your
vaginal muscles so they'll

STRETCH

more easily and perform
to their fullest capacity.

Have what's known as an **active orgasm**. During intercourse, bear down, pushing the same muscles as though you are trying to expel something from your vagina. This helps you to push down against the penis or squeeze it up into you. **The result:** a longer and deeper orgasm. And it'll make his penis stand up and pay attention as well!

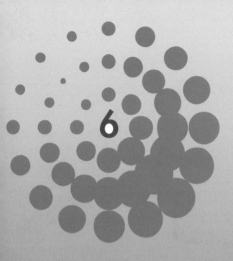

6

Buff **pelvic floor muscles** (the ones you clench when you're desperate for a pee) mean bigger, more intense and just plain **more orgasms** for men and women. Another benefit: the clitoris rests on these muscles, so the exercises also strengthen the clitoris and lead to stronger sensations. Start by squeezing and releasing the muscles 15 times a day, twice each day. Don't hold the contraction; just squeeze and let go. You can do the exercise anywhere: while driving a car, watchingTV, during a meeting. (Just don't announce it to everybody, okay?) Gradually increase the number of squeezes until you're doing about 75, two times a day. (See tip 39 for how to use them during sex.)

7

Working out for around an hour before your sex play gets you hot in every sense of the word. Any kind of vigorous physical exercise helps stimulate the blood flow and boosts aerobic conditioning, which preps the body for a meltdown orgasm. Also, studies show that people who exercise at least three times a week are more in tune with their bodies and more likely to be **sexually responsive**.

SECTION TWO

OH!OH!OH!OH!

SENSORY ORGASMS

You have five built-in tools to help you achieve orgasm — here's how to use them:

8: TOUCHING

The reason why studies find that only 30 per cent of women orgasm during intercourse is because women really need stimulation to the clitoris. But this little magic button is not a minipenis. The best touch? It's one that moves around your love button rather than one that applies pressure directly onto it.

9: SEEING

Seeing: Use your **eyes** as well as your hands and mouth. Just at the moment of orgasm, look deep into each other's eyes. An Archives of Sexual Behaviour study found that the erotic image of your lover in the throes of pleasure is an incredible turn-on for both men and women. You can close your eyes and have an individual experience, but if you keep them open, it's a shared one.

10: TASTE

Chocolate is known to contain natural feel-good chemicals that can boost the sweetness of your orgasm. Smear each other with chocolate body paint and slowly lick it off.

11: SMELL

Women are more sensitive to **pheromones** – substances secreted by the body with an often undetectable odour that stimulates sexual desire.

Nuzzling his armpit during orgasm can give you a heady whiff of his scent that'll make you swoon with bliss.

12: HEARING

If you are going through a lean period **orgasm-wise** or just can't seem to get yourself in the mood, you might want to try role-playing. This is not – repeat not – faking orgasm. Role-playing is when you try to cheer your orgasm into action when it seems to be hovering just around the corner. Exaggerate your movements and sounds – wriggle, clench, moan. Now throw in a few 'yes, baby, yes' screams. The whole idea here is to encourage your responsiveness and cheerlead your orgasm into action.

No-hands Orgasms

According to sex therapists, the best sex starts in the brain...

13 Think that you are enjoying yourself and you will. According to studies by Louisiana-based sex researcher Eileen Palace, PhD, when women learn to raise their expectations about sex, their bodies become more responsive within **30 seconds**.

14 In her research on easily-orgasmic women, Gina Ogden, PhD, found that 64 per cent had experienced orgasm through fantasy or dreams alone, **without any touch**.

15

A Journal of **Sex Research** study found 46 per cent of women and 38 per cent of men regularly indulge in erotic daydreams to keep their love juices flowing.

In fact, in some cases, fantasies made all the difference between experiencing an incredible climax or none at all.

16

Often the reasons for lacklustre orgasms have little to do with our bodies. Cutting out distractions like the phone, work stress and life worries helps you relax, and that helps to speed both your own and your partner's arousal along by widening the arteries of the vagina and penis so blood flows in freely to swell the tissues.

PHYSICAL
FOREPLAY

is an important part of a good sexual experience, but **mental foreplay** is equallly significant. Planning ahead makes your body far more responsive and primes it for orgasm.

18 Concentrate on your own feelings during sex

Women are so often concerned with pleasing their partners or worried about their failure to reach orgasm that they can't fully relax and go with their own flow.

19 Have an emotional orgasm

People think of sex as a very mechanical thing: How big?, how often?, how many times did I have an orgasm?, how long did it take? When we think of sex that way, something is lost – namely, the emotional component that bonds you and your man; the key to sweeter sex. When you catch yourself calculating – what should I do?, how hard? and for how long? – refocus your thoughts and try to concentrate on **how close you feel** to him.

The ultimate no-hands experience is known as the

extragenital orgasm (no vaginal contact). While 10 per

cent of women have this talent naturally, anyone can

develop sexy brain power – just replay your favourite

erotic images in your mind (if you need inspiration, flip

through a sexy magazine). Soon, you'll be able to

mentally bring on the Big O wherever you are.

20

Pleasure Timetable

The timing of a sexual encounter – the day of the month and even the hour of the day – can have a distinct impact on the quality of your orgasms.

21

The **Kinsey Institute** found that only 7.7 per cent of the women whose lovers spent 21 minutes or longer on foreplay failed to reach orgasm.

72

Synchronize your pleasure by giving each other a tongue bath at the same time. Lie head-to-toe and use your mouths as you would your love organs – imitate the grip of your vagina on his penis by contracting and sucking his tool. Meanwhile, he slides a firm tongue in and out of you. Get into a rhythm and then keep it up until you're both swallowed up in mutual ecstasy.

Do it **during your period**. The high levels of progesterone in your body will give you one of the raunchiest orgasms you've ever had. (It's also good for suppressing period pains!)

Right before **ovulation** and around the time you menstruate are two tidal waves of orgasmic energy... get a surfboard and have a fun ride.

Turn 30.

Studies from The Kinsey Institute show that compared to their twenties, when only 23 per cent of women regularly experience orgasm, by 30 around **90 per cent of them do**.

26 As strange as it may sound, many people tend to have sex at precisely the wrong time, physiologically speaking – at the end of the day when they're fatigued, stiff, full from dinner and so least likely to be able to be turned on orgasmically.

27

Testosterone levels are highest when we first wake up, and they decrease as the day progresses, which means your best orgasms are most likely to happen when you make love first thing in the morning.

28

Come first. In one survey of 805 nurses, the women who reported the least trouble in reaching orgasm were those whose partners had delayed their own orgasms until the women experienced theirs. The stop-start technique (every time he is close to orgasm, you stop stimulating him until he can regain control) is one way to slow him down.

DON'T STOP!

MOREGASMS

Or how to have as many moments of pure
bliss as you desire...

29

Women who regularly leap from one
orgasm to another report varied
stimulation is the key. Once
you've climaxed, simply
change the body part being
caressed or your lovemaking
position (and therefore the type
and location of stimulation).

Keep going.

The beauty of the clitoris is that it doesn't need to have any R&R (rest and relaxation) after climaxing. As long as it gets stimulation, you'll keep on coming. (One of the women who took part in a study had a staggering 134 moments of bliss in a row.)

30

A State University of New York Health Science Centre at Brooklyn study found that men can actually learn to climax and keep their erection through three to ten orgasms before exploding in the usual way. The key lies in helping him raise his orgasmic threshold by constantly approaching, then, just before he reaches the point of no return, backing away from ejaculation. Stimulate, then

stop and rest; stimulate, then stop and rest. According to the study, this helps men to separate the sensation of orgasm from the experience of ejaculation. And the physical result? He'll experience all the explosive feelings of orgasm without the ejaculation as often as he desires. And the emotional result? **He'll adore you forever**.

Have a **sequential orgasm**. This means a series of climaxes which come close together – anywhere from one to ten minutes apart – with a slight dip in your arousal in between. Oral sex followed by intercourse is all it takes.

THE ONE-HOUR
ORGASM

Six quick ways to have an endless orgasm...

33 Take a minute to do what you'd normally do in two seconds. Moving in slow motion makes you acutely aware of every sensation.

34

Leaning
away from each
other is perfect for
beginning a love-
making marathon. Sit
on top of your man, facing
him. Now both of you fall
back in opposite directions with
your weight on your elbows or
hands, or lie flat on your back
(whatever makes you happy). He can
gently thrust from below for as long as
your heart's desire (or his penis
holds out) – whichever comes first.

A simple sex surrogate technique called **'vaginal containment'** makes his erection — and your pleasure — last forever. Straddle him or lie on top, with his penis inside you. He shouldn't move at all; he just concentrates on enjoying the sensation of containment without the extra rush of friction.

35

26

Hit the right nerves and sexual euphoria can reach new stratospheres. Research shows that the two genital nerves that surround the pelvic floor muscles give two kinds of erotic sensation. The first is a sharp twinge that occurs when the clitoris or base of the penis is erect and caressed; the second is a warm, melting feeling that happens when the inside of the vagina or the shaft of the penis is stimulated to climatic heights. Experience both types, one after another, in a single love fest, and you'll have what's called a blended orgasm, which can last for as long as an hour. One way is to stimulate one part of body – like the clitoris – until it feels too sensitive to touch,and then move on to the interior of the vagina until it feels aroused, and then return to the clitoris, and so on, and – sigh – on...

37

Recalibrate him. You can teach your man to last longer, plus give him a more explosive orgasm. While stroking his penis with your hand, ask him to rate his arousal on a scale of one to ten, with ten being orgasm. The idea here is to bring him to several peaks and then back down again without him climaxing. When he says he's reached a relatively low four, stop and tell him to breathe until his arousal subsides a hit. Now, rev him up to a heart-pounding eight, then stop until he's back down to a six or so. Finally, take him all the way. Later, he can work the technique into intercourse.

38

Tease yourself. Too many women try
to experience an orgasm as quickly as possible.
Instead, try prolonging your pleasure by
hovering at the brink of orgasm for as long
as possible by building up your arousal and
then getting your partner to shift his loving
attention to a less-stimulating part of your
body for a few minutes. The beauty of this
roller-coaster method is that arousal mounts
to such an intensity that when you finally
let yourself go, you're practically guaranteed
an outrageous orgasm.

NOW! ALL THE RIGHT MOVES...

Most women are well equipped to have an orgasm during intercourse. It's simply a matter of putting yourself in the best position to experience heaven...

39

For a truly explosive orgasm, squat on your partner (who is sitting up). Now thrust towards each other ten times. Stop and then squeeze powerfully with your pelvic floor muscles (see tip 6) ten times.

40

Give his and your love organs a massage in the middle of intercourse for a real orgasmic thrill. Lie back with your legs up, open and wide apart while he lowers himself on you face down, with his head by your feet and his legs over your hips so that his feet are on either side of your shoulders. Then hold onto his hips and pull yourself up a few inches. **Repeat until you collapse.**

41

Factor in the state of your mattress: The softer it is, the more the weight of you and your partner will push your pelvis down and make hitting the most sensitive parts of your vagina less likely. **For best results, try the floor instead.**

Studies have found that 77 per cent of women climax when they use the **coital alignment** technique (also known as the CAT). Your lover climbs on top, à la the Missionary, but instead of entering you straight on, he lies so his weight is totally on top of you and his pubic bone is actually rubbing against your clitoris. By settling into a gentle rocking rhythm, his penis rubs against your clitoris while moving in and out of your vagina.

42

Three simple variations will up your ecstasy odds exponentially when using the Missionary position:

43

Your lover **raises his body**, resting his weight on his elbows or his outstretched arms. This puts greater pressure on your clitoris.

He puts his legs outside yours, while you keep yours together. This will give you lots of friction.

44

45

Raising your legs so that your knees are pressed to your chest and your legs are draped over his shoulders will make your vagina longer, allowing him to penetrate you more deeply. This will give you more friction and pressure exactly where you crave it most of all – your vaginal lips and clitoris.

46

The ultimate hot-spot position:
place two stacks of firm towels together
to form two sets of comfortable piles
a few feet apart. Now face each other so
that your backs are against the pillows.
Arrange your bodies so one partner's legs are wrapped
around the other's and your genitals easily connect. This
position will stimulate multiple erogenous zones for both
of you. You can vary the sensation if he pulls all the
way out on some strokes and rubs his penis against
your clitoris before thrusting in again. And the other
advantage of this position? Four hands free!

SATISFACTION GUARANTEED

These tips promise to please:

At something like 2,000 cycles per minute, the vibrator will send you both so high, you'll need clearance to land. If you don't have access to a sex shop, cheat by getting a battery-powered massager from the chemist. Don't worry about the shape – researchers have found it's the vibrations, not the shape, that triggers orgasm. Place it against your skin near the clitoris (but not directly on it, which can be too painful and intense).

47

48

Making love on a dryer during the spin cycle has a similar effect to using a vibrator.

49

If he tends to come before you and then immediately drops off to sleep, try the **Dual-Stimulation Technique**. Select an intercourse position in which your partner (or you) can easily reach your clitoris (such as the rear entry). This extra bit of stimulation may be all that you need to send you straight to heaven and back.

Lay back and do ... nothing. NOT trying for an orgasm is the surest way to have one.

50

51

After you've **climaxed**, your vagina will tighten up and then contract. If your lover alternates stroking the inside of your vagina with your clitoris, you'll keep on feeling the contractions every five seconds or so until you're completely taken over by delicious waves of pleasure.

52

Get stressed out. Conventional wisdom says that anxiety keeps us from climaxing. Yet there is also evidence to demonstrate that anxiety can increase sexual arousal by wonderfully concentrating the mind – in the same way that pre-curtain butterflies improves an actor's performance.

53

Get out while the sun shines. Just 15 consecutive minutes of exposure to sunlight signals your brain to release the feel-good chemical serotonin, making it easier for you to orgasm when the time comes.

Take charge of
your *pleasure*

We often think of an orgasm
as something which happens to us. Yet all it takes is
a little know-how to control of your own pleasure...

54

You can programme yourself to have a **coital orgasm**
(ie, through intercourse as opposed to clitoral
stimulation) using the Bridge technique. Your partner
(or you) touches your clitoris while he is moving in and
out of you. At the point of your climax, you stop
stimulating and concentrate on the rhythm of his
strokes as you orgasm. Each time you have sex, stop
stimulating your clitoris a little earlier: the penetration
will become the trigger for your mental Big O.

One technique sex therapists recommend to heighten intensity is to hover at the brink of orgasm for as long as possible. Orgasm is really just the release of extreme body tension. So the more tension you have in your body, the more pleasurable the release will be. Savour the bliss of being almost, but not quite there by backing off as you both get close to the Big O. Move to a less-sensitive area for a few minutes, then build the excitement back up again. You can increase and decrease your arousal a few times before surrendering to a head-to-toe burst of pure pleasure.

55

56 **Clenching your buttocks**
and your upper thigh muscles helps increase blood flow
to your entire pelvic area.
This increased blood flow translates into greater vaginal
lubrication and clitoral engorgement, which is believed to
push the nerve receptors closer to the vaginal wall for
greater sensation.
Just be sure not to hold your breath as you squeeze
your behind – it oxygenates the muscles, making your
contractions more efficient.

57

Anything that presses down on part of your lower
abdomen during intercourse (his hand, your hand or
squeezing the muscles or even doing a mini sit-up)
massages your inner clitoris (see tip 71), putting
you over the orgasmic edge.

YES!YES!YES

58

Breathless orgasms... In the heat of passion, how you breathe is probably the last thing you probably want to be thinking about. But, surprisingly, changing your breathing pattern can help increase an orgasm's impact. The **faster** you breathe, the more **excited** you get.

Training the diaphragm, the muscular partition that separates the chest and abdominal cavity, can really increase the intensity of your orgasm. Practise puffing out through your mouth, huff-huff-huff-huff, concentrating on bringing each out-breath up from your belly, so you feel your diaphragm contracting to force the air out. Then during sex, as you feel an orgasm approach, try breathing more strongly and consciously than usual to force each breath out from your diaphragm. You'll increase the tension through your whole abdomen and upper body, raising the intensity of your ecstasy.

59

60

Position yourself so that your head is hanging off the end of the bed. This increases blood flow to your head and changes your breathing pattern, mounting the feelings of sexual tension and arousal.

61

Breathing through your nose is good for de-stressing yourself, but for truly great sex you need to breathe deeply through your mouth.

62

Deep breathing from the stomach instead of the chest during sex will relax you and increase the flow of sexual energy around your body. When you breathe in, push your stomach in as flat as it will go. As you release, push out and hold to the count of five. This makes you feel more energetic, increases your sensitivity to sex and slows down your reactions so you can really take pleasure in them.

Sex therapists advise women who have trouble reaching orgasm to change their breathing patterns. (If you hold your breath, exhale and vice versa.)

63

64

MOUTHWATERING ORGASMS...

Turn your orgasms into a delicious sexperience.

Try teaching him the Zen principle of oral pleasure: You can't 'see' pleasure in a woman, but you can feel it. With this in mind, he should place his tongue flat against your clitoris – the more it pulses, the hotter you are.

65

Remind him that his **tongue** is not a mini version of his penis. He should keep it soft and flat, and think of licking an ice-cream cone rather than plunging it in and out like a hydraulic drill.

66 The average woman needs her lover to spend about 20 minutes 'downtown' in order to make her body salsa.

67

instead of licking, hum – you'll both experience orgasms that will make you vibrate with pleasure!

68 Join your hand and mouth together to hold his penis. Move them up and down in a slow and steady rhythm. This is seriously orgasmic – it will feel like a hot vagina with magic fingers.

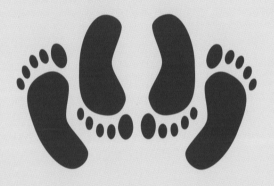

69

Make his entire body curl with pleasure by cradling his penis between your breasts as you lick him.

70 Most men prefer you underneath, like an oral Missionary position. One professional trick is to lie with your head thrown back over the edge of the bed to make your throat form one long, erotic passage.

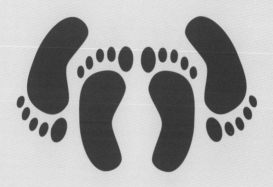

71 Find a rhythm during oral sex. Being in tune with each other's body signals – following breathing patterns, body movements and hip gyrations – will all help to keep you on orgasmic track.

ON-THE-SPOT BLISS

YOU

72 Rather than just a mini-knob of flesh, research published in the Journal of Urology confirms that the clitoris is also composed of around 23 cm (9 in) of highly sensitive erectile tissue that extends along the belly side of the vaginal wall. When stimulated in the right way, this inner clitoris can set off melt-down orgasms.

Best Move: Straddle him and lean back to push his penis against the front wall of your vagina.

The urethra, the tiny area of tissue below the clitoris that you pee from, is actually a sexual pleasure point. **Best Move:** The urethra is a good place to shift his tongue or mouth after you've had an orgasm and your clitoris is feeling too sensitive for continued direct stimulation.

73

74 Achieve maximum pleasure by having him stimulate all three parts of what is called the orgasmic crescent — a curved area that extends from the clitoral tip across the urethral opening (see 73 tip) to the G-spot (see 75 tip).

Best Move: Using tongue, hands or both, your lover should touch both the clitoral tip and the U-spot, while simultaneously pressing the G-spot.

75

The G-spot is a sensitive mass of tissue one-third of the way up the front wall of the vagina (it feels like a soft marshmallow when touched). When pressed, it sets off an orgasm that is deeper and more of a full pelvic wave compared to the quick succession of mini-explosions from a clitoral orgasm.

Best Move: Kneel at the edge of the bed, with your lover standing and entering you from behind.

According to a study published in the Journal of Sex Research, **the cervix** and the clitoris may be part of the same nerve network, which explains why, for roughly half of all women, stimulation of the cervix can lead to an intense orgasm. **Best Move:** Try sitting on top of your partner while facing his feet for the deepest penetration.

The Anterior Fornix Erogenous is on the front wall of the vagina, about one-third of the way down from the G-spot. Research affirms that regularly pressing the area increased overall orgasmic response in the women surveyed, producing more intense – and simply more – climaxes.
Best Move: Lie face-up or sit on the end of the bed while your lover stands between your legs.

The cul-de-sac, found near the cervix, can raise your crescendo of bliss. Once you're aroused, it can be tickled by his penis and the muscles around your uterus will lift up.
Best Move: Make love in the Missionary position. Lift your legs up and back toward your body, sucking your stomach in.

HIM

79 Stroking his frenulum – the vertical ridge that extends from the tip to the shaft of the penis – will hit his climax switch. Not only are there more nerve endings there, but the skin is also extremely thin.

Best Move: Clenching your pelvic muscles just as he pulls out will give his F-spot a massage.

80

Many men are quite
surprised to discover
the range and depth
of the **sensation**
when you stroke
their raphe – the visible
line along the centre of
the scrotum. They
may even end up
ejaculating sooner
than they (and you)
originally planned.
Best Move: Excite
the raphe by gently
running your
fingertips
along it.

81

A man's **erection** doesn't end at the base of the penis. There's a railroad junction full of nerves in the perineum — that smooth triangle of flesh between the base of his penis and his anus which, when pressed, will send him straight into an orgasmic swoon.

Best Move: Gently rub the spot with the pad of your finger or thumb. (Pressing really hard with one forceful push can actually stop him from peaking, so be careful.)

82

Owing to its location at the base of the penis, a man's erection is more or less anchored upon the **prostrate** (also known as the male G-spot).

Best Move: Slip a well-lubricated finger through the rectum and probe the rounded back wall of the prostrate. When you start to feel a firm, rounded walnut-size lump, gently caress it while stroking his penis at the same time.

Both of YOU...

83 The anus is an often-missed hot spot, but it is crammed with sensitive nerves guaranteed to raise the orgasmic quotient.

Best Move: A well-lubricated finger gently slipped into the bottom just as climax hits.

84 Find your hidden hot spot. Make a fist and note where your middle finger hits your palm. Reflexologists believe stimulating this site, which corresponds with the heart centre, helps ignite your orgasm. Before sex, press the spot rhythmically with the thumb of your other hand for 15 seconds, then gently rotate the thumb there for 15 seconds. Repeat three times and then switch hands.

COSMIC SEX

How to achieve joygasmic nirvana:

85 He sits upright with his legs bent at the knees, but wide apart. You sit on top of him with your legs over his while you support his upper body. Now you both move in a rhythmic and slow fashion, while concentrating on deep breathing techniques. According to Taoists, this is the ultimate position to be in while the body orgasms.

Tantrics embrace each other's aura (energy fields said to buzz around each of us) for full-body orgasms. Start by imagining yourselves encircled in a glowing orb of light. Now, facing each other, he puts his Arrow of Love (figure it out) in your Seat of Pleasure as you lie back. Don't move: instead, just concentrate on breathing and looking into each other's eyes. Try to hold out for half an hour — the result will be heavenly.

86

The Karma Sutra describes over 2,000 positions – all

guaranteed to make you explode. Try the Mare, one

of the easier moves. He sits, legs out, and hands behind

him for support. You're on top, with your back to him,

kneeling on either side of his legs.

60-SECOND CLIMAXES

Follow the next few tips and you'll climax before you finish reading this sentence...

88

The moves that work best when you're in a hurry are generally carried out standing up, especially if space is tight. Unfortunately, the male and female physique rarely match up in a way that makes this feasible. Doing it on the stairs (with you one step higher) – or on an incline – evens things out. The same goes for bending over, with your bum towards his groin. In fact, anything done in the Rear Entry position gives the deep penetration often needed for quick sex and lets his penis hit the ultra-sensitive front of your vaginal wall.

89 Some women get an **overwhelming orgasm** from quick intercourse without foreplay, but with deep penetration and they say that it feels different from the orgasms they get from clitoral stimulation or less vigorous intercourse. This sort of orgasm produces gasping, breath-holding, and a once-and-for-all climax. Too much foreplay de-rails this special response, which – when it happens – is as rapid as any man's.

90

In one survey, which was conducted by Bowling Green State University, the majority of women polled reported that they preferred **'hard, driving sex'** to the 'slow, gentle' kind. Researchers concluded that since the vagina is most sensitive in its outer third part, women need to have constant pressure to orgasm during sex.

SECTION SIX

AHHHH!

ORGASM SECRETS

These little-known facts about your orgasms may be just the insider knowledge you need to up your pleasure quotient...

Rest up. When you're exhausted, you just don't have the stamina needed to achieve powerful orgasms.

91

If you're running dry, don't assume you're not interested. You can lubricate without being aroused, and vice versa. Lubrication is influenced by numerous outside factors – your menstrual cycle, whether you drink or smoke, medications like antihistamines and/or how much stress you're experiencing. The simplest solution is to add spit to the mix – yours or his – or water (see 94 tip). Otherwise, invest in a commercial lubricant (note for latex protection users: oil-based products destroy the latex) or condoms with extra lubrication.

92

93

Drink lots of **water** and skip the trip to the toilet before sex. Sex researcher Estelle Lauder, PhD, discovered that many women experience sharp, powerful orgasms as a result of the increased abdominal pressure of a full bladder.

94

Leave the other lubricants and gels in the bathroom cabinet (see 92 tip). Most commercial jellies can be too lubricating and kill the friction needed for orgasm to happen. Use **saliva** or water instead.

95

You've already heard all the boring stuff about the virtues of a balanced diet – but if you **eat right**, your libido functions better. In particular, stock up on anything containing vitamin B (vegetables, eggs, nuts, brown rice and fruit) and zinc (fish, liver, mushrooms, red meat and grains), all of which will enhance the efficiency of the nervous system and hence lead to better orgasms.

96 For orgasmic pursuits, red-light booze. **Alcohol** dulls the nervous system, so while you might want him more after three Cosmopolitans, you'll get much less out of the proceedings.

97 A half-glass of **red wine**, on the other hand, will raise your testosterone levels and will make your reactions even more intense.

98 Speed things up with a double-sided approach. Sex researcher Shere Hite found that 70 per cent of women require clitoral stimulation in order to orgasm. So, combine a finger and a penis, a tongue and a finger, a vibrator and a tongue, then lay back and watch the explosions start!

99

Tobacco constricts the circulation of blood and may lower testosterone – the sex-drive hormone. Both of these are essential for an orgasm. A new study reveals that quitters had more orgasms afterwards than they did when they smoked.

Drink a **coffee** with two sugars.

Since sugar and caffeine increase the heart rate

and give a surge of energy, they can make your

body more responsive to whatever nice things

may be happening to it.

101

Ginseng has been shown to add spice to your orgasms, but make sure you choose your root carefully. Some of the cheaper brands have been shown to contain less than 10 per cent of the potent plant.

102

Orgasms aren't a basic instinct that we're born with – they're a learned talent that comes with practice.

No two orgasms are alike for women. The climatic moment – supreme pleasure followed by a feeling of wellbeing and satisfaction – occurs in the brain's limbic system (or pleasure centre). **Sensations** can range from mild stimulation to an ecstasy so overwhelming that a woman momentarily loses consciousness. Recognize your range as opposed to going for an off-the-Richter Scale even, each and every time.

104

53% of men interviewed for The Janus Report

on Sexual Behaviour replied that their partner's

orgasmic pleasure was more important than their

own, compared to only **34%** of women.

105

Between 10 per cent and 20 per cent of women have experienced a **sleep orgasm**. In that pleasurable experience, they are awakened by an erotic dream culminating in a climax. This is most likely to happen when you have been sexually deprived, but mentally stimulated. For example, he may be out of town, but not out of mind.

106

The average male
orgasm lasts for
10 to 30 seconds;
the average female one
is 13 to 51 seconds.

107

A rich meal eaten just
before making love
can inhibit orgasms.

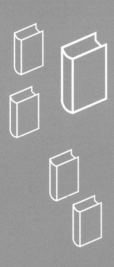

108

Study or get promoted. One survey found that the two best predictors as to whether or not a woman would be able to reach orgasm during sex were education and social standing. Better-educated women with higher professional status were more likely to be orgasmic.

ORGASM BUSTS

Seven things can de-rail your pleasure.
Here's how to get back on track...

109

Problem: Breast-feeding – Prolactin, a hormone
that produces breast milk, dampens your sex drive.

Solution: Think about your baby. The hormone
oxytocin, which releases milk into the breasts, also
stimulates the contraction of the uterine muscles
and may help a woman to climax.

110

Problem: Stress
– Both cumulative and the daily, 'stuck in traffic' kind – can lower testosterone and DHEA, a hormone that enhances sex drive and acts as a mood-booster.

Solution: Before making love, take 20 minutes to re-group (take a walk, change into your playclothes or have a bath).

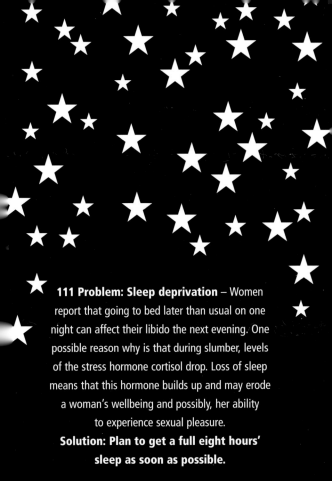

111 Problem: Sleep deprivation – Women report that going to bed later than usual on one night can affect their libido the next evening. One possible reason why is that during slumber, levels of the stress hormone cortisol drop. Loss of sleep means that this hormone builds up and may erode a woman's wellbeing and possibly, her ability to experience sexual pleasure.

Solution: Plan to get a full eight hours' sleep as soon as possible.

Problem: The Pill – By suppressing ovulation, the Pill can lower levels of testosterone and inhibit desire.

Solution: Work with your doctor to play with different levels of progesterone in your prescription.

Problem: The room in which you're making love is illuminated with 175-watt light bulbs.

Solution: Light some candles (but don't leave them unattended!)

114

Problem: You feel self-conscious about your vaginal odour.

Solution: Don't douche. Arousal gives your vagina its own natural muskiness. Look on it as your own custom-made sex perfume. (If it's really unpleasant, though, you may have picked up an infection and will need to get it checked out by a doctor.)

115

Problem: You're scared you'll get pregnant or catch an STD (sexually-transmitted disease).
Solution: Always use a condom. (You should do, anyway!)

116

Problem: You've never had an orgasm.
Solution: Get a blood test. Your anorgasmia (lack of orgasm) may be caused by an injury or abnormal growth on the anterior pituitary gland. Once the lesions are surgically removed, you'll soon become orgasmic.